A
SPOTTER'S
GUIDE

Amazing Architecture

Marvel at the world's coolest constructions – and where to see them

This is Amazing Architecture: classic, quirky, contemporary.

When we travel it's often to see a building – the Taj Mahal, the Leaning Tower of Pisa, the Eiffel Tower. We then photograph ourselves in front of them and, let's face it, the feeling of having claimed these sights is part of the joy of tourism.

But why? Because, buildings are endlessly intriguing: things of beauty, symbols of their age and emblems of human endeavour. As the world's most famous architect Frank Lloyd Wright put it: 'The mother art is architecture. Without an architecture of our own we have no soul of our own civilization.' They speak of ambitions and ideas – and even, occasionally, the basic human need for shelter.

Sometimes, buildings are the reason we decide to go to a place: think of an icon such as Bilbao's Guggenheim and Cambodia's Angkor Wat temple complex. Other times, buildings are less the decoration on the cake than the filling, such as the golden Georgian terraces of Bath in the UK, and the silvery boulevards of Georges-Eugène Haussmann's Paris. From the sublime and the extraordinary to the curious and vainglorious, we've rounded up some of the world's most amazing buildings. You'll find such retro joys as the Atomium in Brussels and the Shabalovka Radio Tower in Moscow, as well as inspirational individualities such as Spain's Dalí Museum.

Among the classics, discover great religious edifices like the Great Mosque of Djenne in Mali, Istanbul's Hagia Sophia, and the UK's glorious Lincoln Cathedral. For cool-hunters, there's Gaudí's Sagrada Familia in Barcelona and the cinematic delights of the Berlin Alexanderplatz TV Tower and New York's Chrysler Building. We've included old favourites and some you may not have seen before.

From the sublime to the strange, join our grand tour of the world's most amazing architecture.

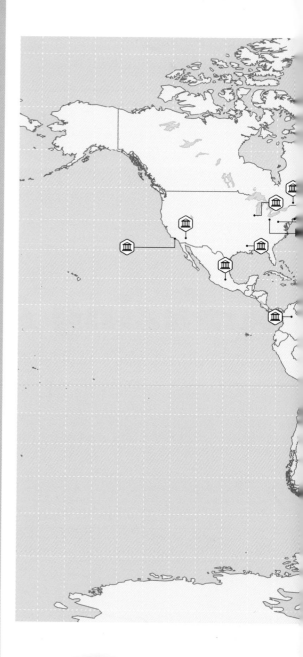

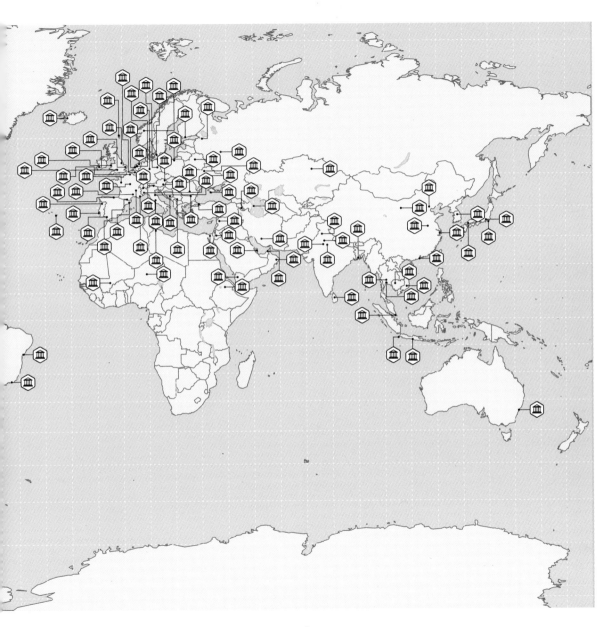

Bahá'í House of Worship

1986

Fariborz Sahba
Delhi, India

Best known as the Lotus Temple, the Bahá'í House of Worship really does look like a huge flower, its petals spread to encourage devotion. The temple is dedicated to the Bahá'í faith – with roots in Shia Islam – and it's open to all. Those 27 white marble 'petals' are free-standing, and nine sides (it's a Bahá'í thing) face into a spectacular central hall large enough to accommodate 2500 people.

In 2001 CNN named it the most visited building in the world. See it in a Delhi sunset and grab yourself a sacred moment.

Our Lady of the Angels Cathedral

2002
Rafael Moneo
Los Angeles, US

There are few new cathedrals in the modern world, but OLA in LA is one. Designed by Spanish starchitect Rafael Moneo, it's been dubbed the world's only 'postmodern' cathedral. Well, it does have some sharp angles and a classic LA site close to the Hollywood Freeway.

But somehow it adds up to a convincing Catholic cathedral – and it even has the relics of 3rd-century martyr Saint Vibiana, resting alongside a more modern icon, Gregory Peck. Nor will its themes of 'Light' and 'Journey' faze the Oprah generation.

Ayutthaya temple complex

c1350

Architect N/A
Ayutthaya, Thailand

There's something thrilling about a lost historic city, and Ayutthaya has that excitement in spades. A world city in the 14th-18th centuries, its position on an island near the Gulf of Siam gave it real trading power.

But they couldn't let it lie. Sacked by Burma, it was abandoned… and the rest is archaeology. But what's left is stunning: elegant 'prang' (reliquary towers) that tease the eye, sturdy monasteries, plentiful preserved murals: all on a grid that speaks of past greatness. Sorry Bangkok… you just don't compete.

Old Bridge (Stari Most)

1566

Mimar Hayruddin
Mostar, Bosnia and
Herzegovina

This 30m hump-backed arch over the river Neretva is a most elegant thing: like a cat stretching over the water below. But Stari Most is also a poignant symbol of reconciliation.

In 1993, the Balkans War took the middle out of the old Ottoman-era crossing, and the two sides of the town, connected for 427 years, were rent asunder. By 2004 it was erected anew, and on baking summer days, the spectacular annual diving competition resumes.

© THIAGO LEITE / SHUTTERSTOCK

Pelourinho

c1550–1600
Architect N/A
Salvador, Bahia, Brazil

The old district of Pelourinho or 'Pelô', in the city of Salvador, has the kind of atmosphere you can slice – not least because, beneath its beauty, it was a place of past atrocity.

Cobbled, steep, and surrounded by colourful Portuguese colonial buildings, including beauties like the light blue baroque Igreja de Nossa Senhora do Rosário dos Pretos, it's UNESCO-listed but utterly alive. Attend one of the huge *bloco* or drum orchestras here on Sundays and you'll hear a defiant link to a difficult past.

The Hermitage (Winter Palace)

1754

Francesco Bartolomeo Rastrelli
St Petersburg, Russia

Once home to the private art collection of Peter the Great, then Catherine the Great, the Winter Palace was the baroque residence of the Russian tsars until it was infamously stormed in 1917. It's still the epitome of bourgeois grandeur, its green and gold façade triumphant in the thin northern light. Within you'll find many of the Hermitage's three million works of art.

Tarry at the Jordan Staircase – it's Rastrelli's masterpiece, with malachite pillars, gilded capitals and cavorting Greek gods. No wonder it enraged the proletariat.

Borobudur

9th century

Gunadharma
Magelang, Central
Java, Indonesia

Rising like a mirage out of dazzling paddy fields, Java's Borobudur is a whopping wonder: an enormous Buddhist complex that hosts a stack of superlatives: biggest Buddhist monument in the world, 504 statues of Buddha, 1,460 narrative panels – indeed, here is the largest and most complete ensemble of Buddhist reliefs in the world.

With a spectacular location in Java's Kedu Valley, the complex has survived earthquakes, volcanic eruptions and war, to remain a place of pilgrimage and prayer.

St Basil's Cathedral

1555

**Postnik Yakovlev/
Ivan the Terrible
Moscow, Russia**

This is *the* symbol of Russia:
a charming conversation
between nine colourful
domes. But it's a bit more
warlike than it seems. Hard
by Red Square, the Cathedral
was built by Ivan the Terrible
to commemorate the
invasion of Kazan. Horrible
fake history also has it that
Ivan blinded its creator,
Postnik Yakovlev, so that
he couldn't make another.
What is true is that religion
was banned here during
Communism and it became
part of Moscow's State
Historical Museum. Fear not.
If you say a prayer now, you
won't end up in a gulag.

Petra

400BC–106AD

The Nabataeans
Petra, Jordan

It's now shallowly defined by its starring role in *Indiana Jones and the Last Crusade*, but Petra is a jolt of deep history and deeper colours. An ancient city carved into the most pinky-red rock you'll ever see, the fabled kilometre-long sandstone Siq (the narrow canyon that leads directly to the famous Al Khazneh, or the Treasury), is the most familiar view, but there's so much more, and as you scramble from tomb to temple, taking in mile upon mile of antiquity, that 'wonder-of-the-world' impact just doesn't stop.

Hagia Sophia

537AD–

**Emperor Justinian
Istanbul, Turkey**

This splendid scarab rising from Istanbul's skyline is one of the world's most important buildings, having served as the centre of Byzantine empire, then an Ottoman mosque, and now a museum. As such it's a romp through the ages, its dome a technological masterpiece that bridges the Roman to the monotheistic era.

When it was completed Justinian is supposed to have remarked 'Solomon, I have outdone thee'. It's not on tape, but perhaps he gets the benefit of the doubt. .

Chapel of the Rosary

1948–51

Henri Matisse
Vence, France

Like an iridescent jewel, this chapel is the masterpiece of Henri Matisse. At the age of 77, the artist created it for a chapter of Dominican nuns, including his former nurse and muse Monique Bourgeois. If the whitewashed exterior is lovely, then the interior is divine: yellow, green and blue stained glass contrasting with black-and-white ceramic murals. Although an atheist, in the Chapel of the Rosary, Matisse created one of the most miraculous religious buildings in the world.

© FRAVAL / SHUTTERSTOCK

Millau Viaduct

2004

Sir Norman Foster (architect); Michel Virlogeux (engineer) Millau, southern France

There's something thrilling about a soaring bridge – and the Millau Viaduct truly soars across the river Tarn as it tumbles through a limestone gorge. So high that it sometimes looks down on clouds, this is bridge-as-hero: tallest bridge tower in the world, highest road bridge in Europe, tallest structure in France. Designed to relieve traffic from France to Spain, it took 17 years to construct. No wonder there was a commemorative stamp. The toll is a mere €7.50, and the gorgeous landscape makes it worth tarrying in the Tarn.

Ring of Remembrance

2014

Philippe Prost
Ablain-St-Nazaire,
Arras, northern France

Properly known as the International Memorial of Notre Dame de Lorette, this is a vast 328m concrete ring on a hill in the Artois region. Created to commemorate the Great War's centenary, within are 500 sheets of steel with 579,606 names in alphabetical order: no creed, country or class mentioned. In a poppy-filled area where French and German troops fought in 1914–15, it's a moving symbol of what Prost calls 'unity and eternity'. Look closer and you'll see that the ring leaves the earth: a reflection of the fragility of existence.

Guggenheim Museum

1997

Frank Gehry
Bilbao, Spain

Two decades ago, American architect Frank Gehry's titanium-scaled masterwork kick-started a whole spree called the Bilbao Effect, in which cities would recover from economic doldrums by way of glittering new arts centres – 'icons', if you will. It was an immediate hit. As well as a gleaming exterior rising like a great fish emerging from a river, the museum's interiors were as dramatic as the astonishing tumble of intersecting titanium panels atop. Tourists came, Bilbao revived, and although it has been much copied, the Guggenheim remains fresh.

Fernsehturm (Television Tower)

1965–69

Fritz Dieter, Günter Franke and Werner Ahrendt
Berlin, Germany

This iconic Berlin tower is *the* great symbol of Cold War Berlin. Built by the German Democratic Republic (GDR) in the 1960s, it chillingly proclaimed 'we're here' – and at 368m, the tallest structure in Germany, soared over Berlin as the perfect metaphor for the age of surveillance.

Nowadays it's part of 'ostalgie' – the city's retro affection for Communism – and you can dine in its restaurant Telecafé, which revolves every 30 minutes.

Chandigarh
Secretariat

1953

Le Corbusier
Chandigarh, India

Chandigarh, the capital of Punjab and Haryana states, is a great place to change trains between Delhi and the northern hill stations. But linger awhile. Planned by the Swiss-French autocrat-genius Le Corbusier for India's first Prime Minister, Jawaharlal Nehru, it is unique in India: a highly planned symphony of roundabouts, squares and extraordinary buildings. One such is this long raw-concrete slab punctuated by a grid of *brise soleils that* keep the interior cool. Outside, Corbu's Open Hand monument completes the picture.

Chrysler Building

1930
William Van Alen for Walter P Chrysler
New York, US

This extraordinary tower mixes a soaring profile, jazzy art deco terraces and gargoyle-like eagles in what was, for just one year, the tallest building in the world; it was trumped by the Empire State Building in 1931. Still, its 318.9m height remain majestic.

Improbably, it's not made of kryptonite but brick wrapped around a steel structure. And as the HQ of the Chrysler Corporation from 1930 until the mid-1950s, it also had to have replicas of Chrysler radiator caps on it. To cap it all, it's still the world's tallest steel-supported brick building.

Yinchuan Museum of Contemporary Art (MOCA)

2015

We Architech Anonymous (WAA)
Yinchuan, China

MOCA opened in the Ningxia Hui Autonomous Region (NHAR) of China with an intention to specialise in Chinese and Islamic art – Yinchuan having been a staging post on the ancient Silk Road. But it's the architecture that surprises, a flowing form said to reflect the Yellow River. So it's a representation of a stream that also offers a bridge between the Arab and Chinese world – a heady, handsome mix of geological and geopolitical forces.

© WAA

© IAN DAGNALL / ALAMY STOCK PHOTO

Fallingwater

1937
Frank Lloyd Wright
Mill Run,
Pennsylvania, US

A tumble of tiers hanging over a creek makes this house look as if it was designed with Jenga. The maestro's 'most beautiful job' (as cited by *Time* magazine on its completion), and a glorious example of his trademark organic architecture, was designed for department store mogul Edgar J Kaufmann and is renowned for its cantilevers over the Bear Run waterway.

A museum since 1964 and a National Historic Landmark, it remains one of Wright's masterpieces, merging home and landscape in a stunning piece of built theatre.

Long Museum
West Bund

2014

Atelier Deshaus
Shanghai, China

This is the first private gallery in China, built for Chinese billionaire Liu Yiqian and his wife Wang Wei. Here the Shanghai-based architects have melded an old coal wharf with a vaulted space – and the mix of raw and old and the polished new really does the business.

As with many other modern-day galleries, the Long Museum is non-linear, allowing the open-jawed visitor to roam freely through the temple-like spaces, marvelling at the smooth-raw contrast.

Qatar Faculty of Islamic Studies

2015

**Mangera Yvars
Doha, Qatar**

It looks like a vast insect, or a new kind of futuristic vehicle, but the Qatar Faculty of Islamic Studies, in Doha's Education City, is in fact a new kind of place of learning – one that melds faith, knowledge and modernity.

As Qatar positions as a culture hub under Her Highness Sheikha Moza Bint Nasser, this building proposes learning in its very fabric, with five large columns representing the five pillars of Islam and Arabic calligraphy taking the message forward in sci-fi manner.

Arquipélago Contemporary Arts Centre (ACAC)

2014

João Mendes Ribeiro + Menos é Mais Arquitectos São Miguel, Azores, Portugal

The Azores may be a brilliant green drop in the ocean, but these days even a remote place needs its iconic gallery – in this case the ACAC. Built around an old alcohol and tobacco warehouse, it's minimal and stark, an effect heightened by the use of grey basalt to mirror the volcanic landscape. It also has workshops and living quarters for resident artists.

© JOSÉ CAMPOS PHOTOGRAPHY

Niterói Contemporary Art Museum

1996

Oscar Niemeyer
Niterói, Brazil

Brazil *is* Oscar Neimeyer. The late architect designed the capital Brasilia, and his Niterói Contemporary Art Museum (MAC), designed when the maestro was 89, is similarly Space Age, with a saucer-like structure poised over Guanabara Bay, a reflecting pool, a curvy red concrete outdoor ramp winding 98m, and (Niterói being part of the Rio de Janeiro metropolitan area) a nearby beach.

Inside what the locals refer to as the UFO, all the furnishings are by Oscar's daughter Anna Maria.

Beijing National Stadium (aka Bird's Nest)

2003–07
Herzog & de Meuron and CAG
Beijing, China

Olympic Games tend to leave a mixed architectural legacy. Some are good, others iffy. The Bird's Nest, the centrepiece of the 2008 Summer Olympic Games, is one of the former, and with artist Ai Weiwei on board, was *the* icon of the Games.

The design was inspired by Chinese ceramics, and those sinuous steel beams hide supports for the retractable roof. The stadium fell into disuse, but now with a mall and concerts, the Bird's Nest will live to tangle once more.

Farnsworth House

1951

Ludwig Mies Van der Rohe, Plano, Illinois, USA

The world's most famous – and influential – holiday home is about to become even more famous as a film star, alongside Jeff Bridges playing irascible modernist genius Mies. The nub is the relationship between Mies and his client, Edith Farnsworth, played by Maggie Gyllenhaal. Farnsworth wanted a second home as a glass-box getaway in which to pursue hobbies, relax and commune with nature. They became lovers then fell out, but left a house that inspired a million transparent extensions.

N 60° 10′ 32.7468′′ E 24° 56′ 0.8772′′

Finlandia Hall

1967–71
Alvar Aalto
Helsinki, Finland

Finland's beauty is not expressive. And the Finlandia Hall – a congress and event venue in central Helsinki – barely whispers its elegance. Aalto designed everything from doors to tiles, and it understandably takes pride of place on the aquatic city's Töölönlahti Bay. With long horizontals and just-so details – not to mention a restaurant and concert hall – the Finlandia Hall feels like a place at peace, like a birch forest or a church. That's genius.

Habitat 67

1967

Moshe Safdie
Montreal, Canada

The capital of Quebec is loveable, with its rinky-dink centre, waterfront and great restaurants. But it's also a Space Age haven thanks to two events: the Winter Olympics of 1976 and the World Exposition of 1967. Habitat 67 arose from the latter, a block of cuboid homes on the Cité du Havre, overlooking the river.

Designed by Israeli-Canadian architect Moshe Safdie to be the Canadian Pavilion for the Expo, the complex experimented with high-quality modular homes in dense urban environments. They still look great, and you can still buy one.

© ANDREW MADALI / 500PX

Burj Al Arab Jumeirah

1999

Tom Wright, Atkins
Dubai, UAE

The Burj is the mascot of Dubai – a luxury hotel that looks like a great sail of an Arab dhow, gazing gulfwards with high hopes. It's a modern legend: the tallest hotel in the world, even (apocryphally) the world's first 'seven-star hotel'. Arrive by helicopter, or via a chauffeur-driven fleet of Rolls-Royces, hit that private beach, and tell your personal butler you'll be having the full Burj. A symbol of modern Dubai.

Sancaklar mosque

2012
Emre Arolat
Architects
Büyükçekmece, near
Istanbul, Turkey

This is a new modernist mosque, a low-lying building that looks as if Frank Lloyd Wright might have been an influence. Almost like a spiritual cave, the Sancaklar mosque works with a series of fractures, as if drawing you into the earth. Any troglodytic effect is alleviated by the combination of light grey stone and sloping terraces outside, harmonising the artificial and natural and evoking, as the architects put it, the 'essence of religious space'.

Heritance Kandalama

1992–95

Geoffrey Bawa
Dambulla, Sri Lanka

Sometimes an architect is a kind of mascot, and Sri Lanka's Geoffrey Bawa, who died in 2003, left an amazing portfolio of buildings, including the Parliament and 13 hotels, all in a 'tropical modern' style. The Heritance Kandalama hotel is one of his masterpieces, and you can stay in it to this day. It is as if a long slab had just emerged from the earth, merging cliff, jungle and cave, with a view of a reservoir and the rock-perched 5th-century royal complex Sigiriya. Enchanting.

© PICS FACTORY / SHUTTERSTOCK

Pompidou Centre

1977
Renzo Piano and Richard Rogers Paris, France

When the Centre Georges Pompidou opened 40 years ago iit was genuinely new and startling – a colourful 'inside-out' boilerhouse particularly noted for its escalators. So celebrated was it that Rogers was parodied in UK satire series *Spitting Image* with his intestines outside his body.

The Pompidou (aka the 'Beaubourg') did more than amuse though; it exceeded all expectations, and with a 'multi-disciplinary' ethos and a space outside full of Interrailing students, it changed the face of the modern art museum.

MMM Corones

2013–15

Zaha Hadid
Mount Kronplatz,
South Tyrol, north-
east Italy

You want a mountain museum to be spectacular – and with a cantilevered platform gazing across the Italian Alps, the Messner Mountain Museum (MMM) Corones delivers. Top mountaineer Reinhold Messner has established six MMMs, but this one is the pinnacle: surrounded by the splendour of the Zillertal, Ortler and Dolomites peaks.

But it's Hadid's building that's the lure: utterly dramatic, with signature curved spaces leading visitors in and out of the mountain itself. At 2275m high, you'll feel the thrill.

La Sagrada Família

1882–

Antoni Gaudí
Barcelona, Spain

The eccentric Gaudí is Barcelona's great mascot and the Temple Expiatori de la Sagrada Família his masterpiece. Towering over Barcelona, it's the exemplar of Gaudí's sinewy gothic-meets-art nouveau style: utterly impressive and vertiginous, and unsurprisingly Spain's most visited monument. Amazingly, it's due to be finished in 2026, 100 years after Gaudí's death, when it will have fully six spires, topping out at 172m to make it the tallest church building in the world.

PARKROYAL
on Pickering

2013
WOHA
Pickering, Singapore

This has to be one of the mightiest flowerpots in the world. Covered in tropical plants – on balconies and terraces inspired by paddy fields and geological formations – this hotel brings a verdant splash into the urban fabric of Singapore.

Every room in the hotel has a green view, and amid the plants are stones, vines and ponds to satisfy the inner Tarzan, as well as a 300m-long garden walk high above street level, all literally topped with an infinity pool and relaxing cabanas. The perfect marriage of town and country.

Kunsthaus Graz

2003

Peter Cook and Colin Fournier
Graz, Austria

One of the results of the European Capital of Culture appellation has been to highlight second cities – and this Kunsthaus, also known as the Graz Art Museum, has really helped to put pretty Graz on the map. Perched between the city's old gables and the river Mur, it works a biomorphic magic with a bubble-like shape and 1066 acrylic glass 'eyes' that twinkle from the its skin.

Graz locals have taken the 'friendly alien' to their hearts and graciously accepted this playful example of 'blob architecture' into the more traditional old town.

© V. BEN / SHUTTERSTOCK

Fuji Television building

1997

Kenzo Tange Associates

Tokyo, Japan

Gazing at this improbable building from the Yurikamome monorail is a fabulously futuristic experience. Hogging the limelight in the waterfront area of the Minato district, it's the HQ of Fuji TV. And it expresses the company's innovative nature in no uncertain terms, with a lattice of 'sky corridors' holding a 32m titanium silver ball in place.

Climb to that ball and you'll see fantastic views of Tokyo to one side and Mount Fuji to the other. Bizarre and beautiful.

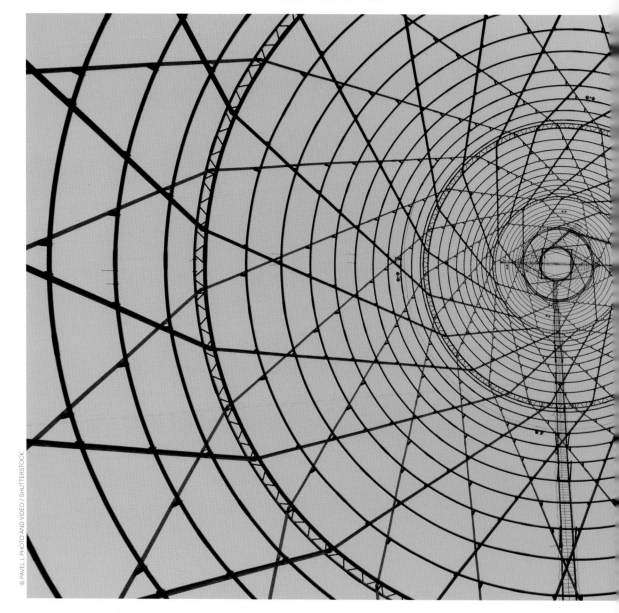

Shabolovka (aka Shukhov) Radio Tower

1920–22
Vladimir Shukhov
Moscow, Russia

The Russian Revolution left an avant-garde architectural legacy, and a great survivor is Vladimir Shukhov's Shabolovka Radio Tower, known informally as Russia's Eiffel Tower.

Technology-wise it's a milestone: a hyperboloid steel structure stacked up into a skywards cone aiming to reach 350m – it only made it to just over half that height at 160m. In 2014 there were demolition plans which have been headed off with a preservation order; if you can't get to Moscow to see it, there's a model at London's Science Museum.

Atomium

1958

André and Jean Polak (architects); André Waterkeyn (engineer) Brussels, Belgium

The country that gave us René Magritte is full of surreal surprises. But the Atomium – a building in Brussels made to look like the cell of a crystal, with 'atoms' connected by air bridges – surely takes the waffle. Constructed for the 1958 Brussels World's Fair, Expo 58, it's now a retro treat and at 103m high, surprisingly big. Inside, a warren of stairs, escalators and nodules awaits, including a great view of Brussels. A wonderful curiosity, with a pleasing message of world peace and economic progress.

© MARGARET STEPIEN / LONELY PLANET

Metropol Parasol

2011

Jürgen Mayer
Seville, Spain

It could be said to be art, not architecture. But the Parasol is definitely a building, soaring over Seville's once-tired Plaza de la Encarnación, and, at 150x70m, the largest wooden structure in the world. It was controversial, took ages, cost double its original budget and gained the inevitable nickname Las Setas de la Encarnación – 'incarnation's mushrooms'. But as a device to cover a market, provide shade, create museum space and offer tourists a panoramic walkway atop, the Finnish birch-made Parasol is spectacular.

Portmeirion

1925–76

Clough Williams-Ellis
Gwynedd, north Wales

How to describe this fantasy village: a drop of Tuscan-meets-Tyrol-meets-Disney in the unlikely environment of the Dwyryd estuary on the west coast of north Wales? As a delightful and visionary confection by architect Sir Clough Williams-Ellis perhaps; and one that would never pass through a planning process today.

Taking more than 50 years to build, Portmeirion is still best known in the UK from its role in the 1960s TV oddity *The Prisoner*, so it's delightful to find that it not only exists, but is a successful working resort with hotels, cafes and restaurants.

© PICASA / GETTY IMAGES

Palais Stoclet

1905–1911

Josef Hoffmann
Brussels, Belgium

This stately villa stands incongruously in a suburb of Brussels and is a fascinating historic capsule.

In 1905 Banker and art collector Adolphe Stoclet commissioned Hoffman to bring the ultra-fashionable art of the Vienna Secession to northern Europe, resulting in this geometric gem.

Not all warm to its icy Norwegian marble exterior, but with 20ft murals by Gustav Klimt, opulent onyx, parquetry, marble and mosaics inside, it's undeniably grand – and sadly off-limits, as it's privately owned.

Basket building

1997

WOHA
NBBJ
Newark, Ohio, US

This is the building-as-selfie opportunity: a seven-storey folly that looks exactly as it says it looks. The 'Big Basket' is a retail building that belonged for a long time to an interior decor company which, ahem, sold baskets. Thus did boss Dave Longaberger suggest that it should look like one of its baskets, and history was made – using locally sourced Ohio wood.

It's changed hands since, but the Basket building remains in a proud American tradition: buildings that look like what's on sale in them.

© SAIKOSP / SHUTTERSTOCK

Heydav Aliyev Centre

2007–12
Zaha Hadid
Baku, Azerbaijan

Oil-rich Azerbaijan is keen to out-wow the Gulf from its out-there location on the Caspian Sea. So mega-starchitect Hadid won the competition to design the ruling Aliyev family's museum, and this is the incredible result.

The killer view is from the south, where the vast form rises like a peaking graph – one of Hadid's signature 'biomorphic' curves – while inside, the wide white stairs and misty sightlines make you think you've gone to high-drama heaven, somewhat dwarfing the exhibits.

Konstantin
Melnikov house

1929
**Konstantin Melnikov
Moscow, Russia**

One hundred years ago, the Russian Revolution was steaming ahead. Out with the old! The new era needed a new look, its own architecture, to herald the brave new world. Hence, this two-cylinder house with 60 hexagonal windows by architect-artist Konstantin Melnikov, inspired by a honeycomb and intended to house his family and studio. You'll have to hunt for it in Moscow's Arbat district, but it's worth it – another great survival of the Russian avant-garde.

Cube houses (Kubus Woningan)

1977
Piet Blom
Rotterdam,
Netherlands

It's exhilarating, in a childlike way, to see a house on its side, and these 38 yellow cube houses above the Blaak Station in Rotterdam certainly captivate the imagination.

Blom conceived the design of each house as a tree, and their collective bulk a forest, and they're certainly striking outside: a tumble of squares that make you look anew at the world, as if through a kaleidoscope. They're fun inside, too, with dramatic spaces giving views over Rotterdam. One enterprising resident even offers tours.

Palácio Nacional da Pena

1836

Wilhelm Ludwig von Eschwege and Nicolau Pires
Sintra, Portugal

This castle is one of Europe's high romantic moments: all painted terraces, gargoyles, battlements and statues taking full advantage of a great setting. The zigzag walk up the hill – particulary when misty –is hugely atmospheric.

Atop, the Palácio is a flamboyant confection commissioned by Ferdinand August Franz Anton from Austria, who married into the Portuguese royal family. The Royals have longe gone, but the sense of extravagance lingers on.

Rietveld Schröder house

1924

Gerrit Rietveld
Utrecht, Netherlands

The best thing about this cubic house is that it's so unexpected, tucked away in a side street in Utrecht. Built by Rietveld for Truus Schröder-Schräder and her children, his big idea was to design it without walls so that one could change it whenever one wanted.

By all accounts the build saw a lot of blood, sweat and tears – and a client-architect affair – but now, with sliding and revolving panels making it a dynamic, fluid family space, it's revered as a fine domestic expression of the avant-garde art movement De Stijl. Cranky but charming.

© VLADIMIR ALEXEEV / ALAMY STOCK PHOTO

Rock churches

13th–14th centuries

Architect N/A
Ivanovo, Bulgaria

There's something elemental about a rock church, and Ivanovo's beauties are a real find. You'll drive to sleepy Ivanovo, then hike to the churches, which are indeed carved into the rock. Cooling off inside, you can then marvel at the amazingly fresh medieval frescoes, and ancient graffiti too.

Even the names are great – St Archangel Michael Chapel (the Buried Church), the St Theodore Church (the Demolished Church) – and afterwards, you can hike through the rest of the Rusenski Lom Nature Park.

Jantar Mantar
Observatory

1724–30

**Maharajah Jai Singh II
Jaipur, Rajasthan,
India**

Most buildings have some recognisable shape – a house, an office, a bridge. Not so the Jantar Manta Observatories. This group of five astronomical parks plunges the visitor into a hallucinogenic world of strange predictive cosmology.

Jai Singh II created the five Jantar Mantars in northern India and this one, at Jaipur, feels the most otherworldly, its influences drawn from all different religious and social beliefs in order to create no fewer than 19 astronomical instruments.

© TANJALA GICA / SHUTTERSTOCK

Hiroshima Memorial

1915

Jan Letzel
Hiroshima, Japan

There are few modern ruins as poignant as this. The Hiroshima Peace Memorial (also known as the A-Bomb Dome) is the symbolically empty and decrepit centrepiece of Hiroshima's Peace Memorial Park.

Built as an arts and exhibition centre in 1915, it was part of the conflagration of 6 August 1945 that immediately took the lives of 70,000 people. As the building was the only thing left standing it was – after some conflict – kept as an elegiac reminder of the event.

Eiffel Tower

1879–89
Gustav Eiffel
Paris, France

The beloved iron tower is one of the world's most instantly recognisable monuments – and it still causes jaws to drop at first sight. Built to commemorate the French Revolution, the 324m-high La Dame de Fer was the tallest structure in the world until 1930.

Yes, visitors quickly learn about the terrible queues and the tat touts beneath – after all, about seven million people visit a year – but there's no gainsaying its immensity. The tower survived Hitler and has become a canvas for illuminations, celebrations and commiserations: a beacon to the world.

Bayterek Tower

1996-2002
Akmurza
Rustembekov
Astana, Kazakhstan

It looks like a giant World Cup trophy – and indeed, Bayterek is the football team of Astana. But this giant observation tower actually represents a Kazakh myth: that a magic bird called Samruk laid an egg in the tree of life.

If that sounds a bit Borat, climb the monument to look out over this increasingly prosperous country, and ponder that the 97 metres you're climbing represents the inauguration of Astana as Kazakhstan's capital in 1997. While there, you can put your hand in an imprint of President Nazarbayev's hand and make a wish.

© COURTESY OF SCDA ARCHITECTS

Sky Terrace

2015

SCDA Architects
Singapore

These five towers were built as most towers are: to cope with the eternal problem of fitting more people into a limited space. But they are no average blocks. They're solar-powered, with rainwater harvesting and drip irrigation, as well as natural ventilation in all the apartments.

The green bridges make it look as if they're holding hands, roof gardens and playgrounds are meant to help residents connect with eachother, and even the flats within can be connected: the purpose being to create a 'multi-generational vertical village' with energy-efficiency and social interaction in mind. A vision of the future? Hopefully.

Robert Tatin Museum

1962-83

Robert Tatin
Frénouse, Cossé-le-Vivien, France

This charmingly whacky museum is a labour of love by artist-architect Robert Tatin, who bought the house in 1962, then augmented his collection of Neolithic art with huge, numinous sculptures, marrying the Gallic past with world religions, legends and history: dragons and gods – as well as Joan of Arc and Pablo Picasso.

Even the garden path is flanked by huge stone figures as if Easter Island and the Aztecs had dropped in on rural France. Oh, and Tatin is buried near the entrance to his life's work.

© PETE SEAWARD / LONELY PLANET

Sydney Opera House

1973

Jørn Utzon (later Peter Hall)
Sydney, Australia

So often have its interlocking shells been photographed that Sydney Opera House is both emblem of and gateway to Australia.

In pole position on Bennelong Point, the arts institution's concrete carapaces were an engineering masterstroke, but the building was hard-won. Danish architect Utzon designed it in 1957, but epic costs, delays and Utzon's 1966 resignation took their toll. Nevertheless, it worked: a national symbol that eight million people visit each year, and UNESCO status to boot. Perhaps it was worth going 1,357% over budget...

Sana'a 'skyscrapers'

8th–13th centuries
Architect N/A
Sana'a, Yemen

They're known as the earliest 'skyscrapers' in the world: grand houses of up to 12 storeys improbably but robustly made from mud and adobe bricks, and exquisitely patterned with elaborate friezes, filigreed roofs and stained-glass windows.

Pioneered by the early Ād tribe, like all skyscrapers they became a bit of a 'beat the Jones's' contest. As each family grew, new storeys would be added, the whole lot supporting an ecosystem of domestic agriculture. Sadly, they've been damaged by recent military action and visiting is not advised.

Hotel Rogner
Bad Blumau

1997
Friedensreich
Hundertwasser
Styria, Austria

This bizarre apparition – all multi-coloured domes, bulging pillars, golden mosaic trees pressed into walls and wobbly skylines – is the instantly recognisable work of artist, architect and eco-philosopher Hundertwasser, whose hippy-meets-Klimt signature style enjoys an enormous following. Inside the 46-room hotel and spa, higgledy-piggledy corridors and curved floors follow his notion that there are no flat floors in nature, and the effect is pleasing disorientation: like staying in a prog-rock album cover.

Grand Lisboa

2008

Dennis Lau and
Ng Chun Man
Sé, Macau, China

One day, there'll be a special prize for 'excessive casino architecture' – and it may well be that this pile in Macau pips Vegas. With a head like a lotus hovering over a ball – or is it a Brazilian headdress? – this extraordinary landmark is sometimes called 'postmodern', placing it into an almost respectable historic category. But it's in a class of its own; intended to 'embody the unique vitality and spirit of Macau', its flamboyant exuberance tops out at 30,000sq metres of casino space, making it the biggest building in Macau.

© GORAN BOGICEVIC / SHUTTERSTOCK

Nakagin Capsule Tower

1972

Kisho Kurokawa
Ginza, Tokyo, Japan

This 1970s classic was thought to herald the future when it was built, taking the form of a lot of small bedrooms – capsules – that were intended for Japan's army of salarymen, who would sleep in central Tokyo during the week. Each of the 140 4m x 2.5m modules can be replaced, and it's all set in two interconnected towers which, combined, resemble a huge cuboid beehive. Has it worked? Well, only about 30 are still inhabited, the water's been cut off, and there's talk of demolition, so probably not – but the 'Save Nakagin Tower' campaign might well see this cultural curiosity live on.

Ryugyong Hotel

1987–

Baikdoosan Architects & Engineers Pyongyang, North Korea

This is the pride of Kim Jong Ils Kim Il-sung's secretive state – well, kind of; the vast and striking 330m steel pyramid remains unfinished and empty 30 years after it was started. Its name, the curiously bucolic 'capital of willows', belies its bombastic scale and ambition – 105 storeys of mixed-use space, including a 3000-room hotel – but it's the more common name of the 'Hotel of Doom' that best reflects its tough stop-start journey of missed deadlines– the first being the 13th World Festival of Youth and Students in June 1989.

Bank of Asia Robot Building

1987

Sumet Jumsai
Bangkok, Thailand

Architect Sumet Jumsai's brief was to design a building that reflected 'the modernisation and computerisation of banking'. The muse hit him when he saw the toy robot belonging to his son. What ensued was a bank that really does look like a sci-fi robot, complete with two antennae on the roof and doleful large eyes... but that's not the only reason to love it. The architect himself had high-minded ideals: to create a building that reflects the 'contemporary amalgamation of human and machine'. Go robot.

Hang Nga Guesthouse (Crazy House)

1990

Đặng Việt Nga
Đà Lạt, Vietnam

Some liken it to a fairy tale – if that's the case, it's one of those Grimm ones in which children get eaten. The Hằng Nga guesthouse is like a mash-up of Gaudí, Dalí, Tolkein and Disney: all sinuous twisted forms with hardly a right angle to be seen. With ten animal-themed guest rooms, each with uneven windows, connected by tunnel-like corridors, the whole effect is organic, enchanting and slightly sinister. The local People's Committee haven't always like it, but tourists flock to this unique bothy in lovely, artsy Đà Lạt.

The Ideal Palace (Le Palais Ideal)

1912
Ferdinand Cheval
Hauterives, France

This historic example of Outsider (that is, untrained) art, also known as naïve art architecture, is a monument to the creativity of a French postman. Ferdinand Cheval, who took 33 years to build his Ideal Palace. During his daily 18-mile postal round, Cheval collected stones and slowly but surely created his incredible temple, which was recognised by Picasso, Max Ernst and the surrealist André Breton, and now belongs to the Peggy Guggenheim Collection. Ffittingly, the artist-postman was honoured on a postage stamp in 1986.

Angkor Wat

12th century
Suryavarman II
Siem Reap, Cambodia

Angkor Wat is the biggest temple complex in the world. It took an estimated 300,000 workers and 6,000 elephants to bring the sandstone blocks from Phnom Kulen, some 25 miles away. With that stone came the perfect city: a theological representation of sacred Mount Meru, where the Hindu gods do dwell, and a host of temples and statues as well as roads and canals.

Angkor is a lesson in city planning as well as a religious site, and the centre of the Khmer empire, which ruled much of what today is Cambodia, Thailand, Laos, and southern Vietnam.

You could spend months here. As Lonely Planet's top sight in the world, it's a bucket-lister to end them all.

© ARCAID IMAGES / ALAMY STOCK PHOTO

Central Concert Hall

2009

Manfredi Nicoletti
Astana, Kazakhstan

Another building-as-flower – although this time, it could be a predatory flytrap, with concentric walls enclosing a gaping maw. That said, it's impressive: covered in turquoise tiles and another mega-icon from the go-ahead Central Asian republic, it opened a few years ago to bring a splash of culture to the steppe. Inside is an enormous concert hall and a great civic space – like a covered public square – that enfolds the good people of Astana throughout the entire year and has a panoply of restaurants, shops, and bars.

National Library of Belarus

2006

**Viktor Kramarenko
and Mihail Vinogradov
Minsk, Belarus**

This library is pride of place in Europe's most enigmatic nation – and it means a lot to them. More than a mere collection of books, the library is a national landmark and its importance is underlined by its diamond shape – or if you're feeling more particular, a rhombicuboctahedron.

Within you'll find reading rooms, a book museum, and an observation point, while outside the architectural bibliophilia continues with an entrance in the shape of an open book and a statue of the Belarussian hero of printing, Francisk Skorina.

Lincoln Cathedral

1073–

Bishop Remigus /Hugh of Avalon Lincoln, England

It's only the third biggest of the English cathedrals, but many (including John Ruskin, who called it the most precious piece of architecture in the British Isles') think it the best. Perhaps it's the three towers that look over the flatlands – in 1311, it pipped the Great Pyramid of Giza to be the tallest building in the world – or the setting at the top of quaint Steep Hill, or the rich collection of Anglo-Medieval art, including one of the four copies of Magna Carta. An English dream.

Taj Mahal

1632–53

Shah Jahan and Ustad Ahmad Lahauri

Agra, India

The Mona Lisa of the built world, in the (marble) flesh the Taj never disappoints: the serenity, the symmetry, the scale… it's the world's loveliest tomb. Mughal Emperor Shah Jahan truly loved one of his significant others, Mumtaz Mahal, above all else, and when she died in 1631 he wasn't going to forget her. Mustering 22,000 labourers and craftsmen and 1000 elephants, the Shah finished her tomb more than 20 years later, only to be subject to a coup. He now lies in the Taj himself: and some of its poignancy was revived when Lady Diana used the Taj as a photocall in 1992.

Hôtel Tassel

1892–1894

Victor Horta
Brussels, Belgium

Brussels is the world centre of the curvaceous architectural and decorative style art nouveau, and Horta is its prime exponent. Not yet as florid and ornate as the style would become, the Hotel Tassel was designed for the scientist Emile Tassel and is considered the first glimmer of nouveau, which began to sprout into the 20th century with increasing flamboyance.

Horta designed everything in the building, from stained glass to doorknobs and mosaic floors to woodwork, and a visit will leave you appreciating the hidden charms of the Belgian capital.

Great Mosque of Djenné

Originally 13th century, current structure 1907

King Koi Konboro
Djenné, Mali

Mud, mud, glorious mud: the Great Mosque of Djenné is the most atmospheric adobe building in the world, and the biggest. Towering over the crossroads city, it surrounds the mud-built homes like a queen bee. The mosque's original build dates back to the 13th century but is ongoing and never-ending, and an annual festival called La fete de Crepissage (Plastering) is a ritual necessity after the rainy season in May, when all the town's inhabitants come together to reapply the clay lost during the monsoon.

© VIEW PICTURES LTD / ALAMY STOCK PHOTO

Balancing Barn

2010
MVRDV
Suffolk, UK

Built for an innovative architecture-focused homestay company called Living Architecture, the 30m-long Balancing Barn's big feature is its extraordinary 15m cantilever, which looks precarious but is safe as houses – so much so that they've put a cute swing on the grass slope beneath it, adding to the impression that you're staying in a vast seesaw. Near a nature reserve, the Barn's silver tiles contrast nicely with the green, low-lying landscape over which the house gazes.

Nanchang Wanda Mall

2016
Wanda
Nanchang, China

It's not just economics, stupid. China is also challenging America's supremacy in themed architecture. Take this mall in the southeast city of Nanchang, which mimics a giant tea ceremony. Part of a theme park called Wanda Cultural Tourism City, the mall simulates the fabled Qing Dynasty's blue and white porcelain, which was produced nearby. Marvel at the imagery of animals, plants and landscapes – painted, in the Chinese spirit, to be full of good fortune – then enter those Brobdingnagian cups to find a bewildering array of shops, attractions and hotels.

© IAIN MASTERTON / ALAMY STOCK PHOTO

Palace of the Parliament

1984
Anca Petrescu
Bucharest, Romania

It's in questionable taste but this has to be included for scale alone – the world's second-largest single-building footprint after the Pentagon. Built by deposed despot Nicolae Ceauşescu in a serve- chilled neoclassical style, it has more than 3000 rooms, and the 'Conducător; made sure its driveway – the Victory of Socialism Boulevard (now Boulevard Unirii) was wider than the Champs Elysees. A megalomaniacal masterstroke, 'The People's House' also involved razing historic Bucharest, a process known as 'systematisation'.

Turning Torso

2005

Santiago Calatrava
Malmö, Sweden

Coming on like a tower block suffering a Chinese burn, the Turning Torso is in Malmö's Western Harbour, near the Öresund bridge connecting Sweden with Denmark, and is a classic bit of post-industrial waterside regeneration. Forged as part of a European housing exhibition, it is the world's first twisted skyscraper: a jeu d'esprit typical of jokey Calatrava, akin to the figura serpentinata of Renaissance art. Standing brashly at 190m, it annoyed the sober Swedes, and replaced a much-loved crane in this ship-building city, but has served well as a gatepost to Sweden.

Monte Rosa Hut

2009

**Andrea Deplazes of
ETH Zurich
Zermatt, Switzerland**

Location, location and... wow. This minimal mountain refuge looking like a dark rock crystal is almost part of the geology of this astonishing landscape. At 2883m the Monte Rosa Hut offers high-altitude hospitality for hikers and mountaineers. Run by the Swiss Alpine Club, it has views of the Alps' highest peaks, including the Matterhorn, although you'll need to be fit to make it as far as this silvery aluminium bothy. If you do, 120 beds and one of the world's best observation decks await.

Bran Castle

1377–1382

**Hungarian king
Louis I and others
Transylvania, Romania**

We all know this place in our mind's eye; as Dracula's fortress in Bram Stoker's 1897 novel Dracula. Or is it? Stoker never visited Romania, and it's thought he based it on descriptions of this castle on the Bran Gorge, augmented by his fiendish imagination. It doesn't matter, as Bran Castle is inextricably linked with the vampiric legend and has the tourism industry to show for it. The red-roofed castle does look properly scary. Brooding, asymmetric and Gothic, it's the embodiment of clifftop eyrie as a place of ghoulish entrapment. Few would stay here without garlic and stake.

Sculpture-habitacle n°2

1964

**André Bloc
Meudon, France**

There's a distinguished strand of houses designed by artists, and this 'habitable sculpture' by French polymath creative André Bloc – artist, architect, engineer and journalist – is a fine example. Bloc's curious construction was designed when he was 68 and had all but given up architecture to concentrate on sculpture. His mission? To get the world to realise that 'the works of urban planners and architects reach a banality of desperation'. It's been classed as a historic monument since 1983.

Casa Terracota

2012

**Octavio Mendoza
Morales**

**Villa de Leyva,
Colombia**

This huge hunk of pottery is the life's work of environmental activist Mendoza, who built it by hand in a Colombian mountain village, baking the clay in the sun and using recycled junk for many of the fittings. The theme continues inside with clay tables and clay utensils across its two storeys. With a great mountain-view location, Mendoza's ethos was to create harmony between the land and community, and to 'transform soil into habitable architecture'. So the fact that locals call it the 'Casa de Flintstone' won't faze him.

National Public Library of Kosovo

1982

**Andrija Mutnjaković
Pristina, Kosovo**

Pride of place in one of the world's newest capital cities, Pristina's library, with its stacked cubes and 99 white domes, has been controversial, with some likening it to a prison. It's certainly striking, and all manner of theories have sprung up about its symbolisms – the domes representing the national Albanian hat, the plisi, being one of the more fanciful ones. Mutnjaković himself has said that the library blends Byzantine and Islamic architectural traditions: important symbolism in this contested country.

Odeillo solar furnace

1970

Felix Trombe

Font-Romeu-Odeillo-Via, France

This amazing structure, like a huge domestic heater, is the world's largest solar furnace. With a combined near-10,000 mirrors focusing the sun's rays back to a single point, it gets hot – about 3500°c – so French chemist Trombe's solar furnace is used by researchers and agencies like NASA to assess the effects of high temperatures on materials, as well as to study solar energy.

Set in a lovely landscape, it's a remarkable place to visit, and has an information centre where visitors can learn about the benefits of harnessing the sun's power.

Nord/LB Building

2002

**Jan LetzelBehnisch,
Behnisch & Partners
Hanover, Germany**

This building looks as if a child played with some building blocks then sent a picture to the builders. And nothing wrong with that, for as a bank building it's uncharacteristically fun. A series of articulated steel and glass boxes, sometimes propped with pillars, it's a real eye-catcher. The staff restaurant has a butterfly wing roof, and a tower features lights that change colour with the sun's position. Plus it's as energy-efficient as you'd expect from a German building, with a design that optimises the use of natural ventilation and daylight.

The Crooked House (Krzywy Domek)

2004

**Szotyńscy & Zaleski
Sopot, Poland**

As if to show how the mundane can become marvellous, the Crooked House is a building on a normal shopping street in this seaside town, and it hosts a mall with restaurants, shops and businesses.

Rather than go the normal route, however, the architects – inspired by Polish children's book illustrator Jan Marcin Szancer – went for a wonky fairytale route, distorting all the house's lines to bizarre and comic effect. Sopot's tourists love it – although some still fear entering.

Dalí Theatre-Museum

1974

**Salvador Dalí
and others
Figueres, Spain**

We all know about Dalí, the moustachioed depicter of melting clocks, but this museum (and mausoleum – Dalí is buried here) renew our acquaintance in delightful fashion. From the outside, it looks like a red castle, decorated with eggs and chess pieces and topped with a huge geodesic dome. Built on the site of an old theatre, it's a splendid addition to (in Dalí's own words) 'the new, unsuspected and hallucinatory world of Surrealism'. If you get the surreal bug, take the half-hour journey to his coastal house in Port Lligat.

Druzhba Holiday Centre

1984

Igor Vasilevsky
Yalta, Ukraine

One from the James Bond baddie school of architecture, this cylindrical Holiday Centre on Ukraine's Black Sea has that Cold War space-race aesthetic down pat – indeed, legend has it that in those febrile years, the US thought it was a new and sinister military building. Perched on a hill, and supported by legs and trusses, guests enter via a glass tube. All the rooms are oriented to get a good view, hence that prickly hedgehog look. A late Soviet gem.

The Calakmul building

1997

Agustin Hernandez Navarro
Mexico City, Mexico

You can see why locals immediately christened this handsome cube 'La Lavadora' – the Washing Machine. But its real intent was to reference Mexico's Mayan past, both in its name Calakmul, a Mayan region, and in a kind of animist honouring of earth and sky. It's also joined by a pyramidal neighbour, offering a pleasing interplay of geometric shapes that extend the impression of a globe inside a cube created by the mirrored glass of the main nine-storey structure.

Mammy's Cupboard

1940

Architect N/A
Natchez, Mississippi, US

If you find yourself on Highway 61, which tracks the Mississippi river from Memphis to the Gulf Coast, you'll see many strange things, including Mammy's Cupboard, which may look funny, but hasn't always been.

This roadside restaurant is a classic piece of mid-century Americana, made as a tourist attraction when the 'Aunt Jemima' archetype of an African American woman was considered an innocent bit of minstrelsy. That all changed, and a solution came with the 1960s and the Civil Rights Movement – paint Mammy's skin pink.

The Egg

1966–1978

**Harrison & Abramovitz
Albany, New York, US**

The Egg is an early example of a now familiar idiom – the arts icon that grabs the limelight for a town. In this case the Egg was hatched as part of Nelson Rockefeller's Empire State Plaza government complex.

Ovoid, tilted on an axis and perched on a pedestal, it's a real eye-catcher. Within there are two theatres, and a stem that descends six storeys. The reinforced-concrete whopper is much-loved by locals, and NY band They Might Be Giants even wrote a song about it in 2004.

Shoe House

1949

Mahlon Haines, Hellam, Pennsylvania, US

Another fine piece of roadside Americana, the 25ft Shoe House was built by shoe salesman Haines, aka the 'Shoe Wizard', as a promotional tool. Legend has it that Haines gave an architect an old boot and said 'Build me a house like this'. There's something eccentrically brilliant about the house's shoe mailbox, shoe decorated fence and stained glass windows depicting shoes. There's even a little shoe-shaped doghouse nearby. That its location is now called Shoe House Road must have pleased Haines greatly.

© DP PHOTOGRAPHY / SHUTTERSTOCK

Chapel of the Holy Cross

1956

Richard Hein and August K Strotz
Sedona, Arizona, US

'Don't forget Sedona', runs the line in the great R&B song 'Route 66', and if you are passing by, spare a moment for the Chapel of the Holy Cross. As if rising from from the red rocky buttes, the chapel was the brainchild of sculptor Marguerite Brunswig Staude, a student of Frank Lloyd Wright who was inspired by a vision of a cross on the Empire State Building. After a couple of false starts, she found the site in Coconino National Forest. It's genuinely impressive, rising 76m high from the 305m cliff, and has great views from inside, too.

Rumah Miring (Slanted House)

2015

Budi Pradono
Pondok Indah,
Jakarta, Indonesia

Who says a house has to be, you know, straight up and down? This handsome house in an upscale suburb of Jakarta was described by the architect as 'anti-establishment' and is a clear riposte to its plush neighbours, who've largely opted for pillar-and portico grandeur. With a tilted steel frame and oodles of glass over three floors, it's really married a sense of play with a feeling of high-tech luxury. Its owner, gallerist Christiana Gouw, called it a 'celebration of individual freedom'.

Crac des Chevaliers (and Qal'at Salah El-Din)

1142–1271

Architect N/A

Near Homs, Syria

This flat-topped behemoth was once the most important building in the world and a technological marvel, bringing the best of Byzantine and Frankish building into a fortress that was said by TE Lawrence to be 'perhaps the best preserved and most wholly admirable castle in the world'. The Syrian civil war puts it out of bounds at the moment, sadly, and it is thought that the Crac has sustained some damage.

Borgund Stave Church (Apostle Andrew church)

c1250

Architect N/A
Borgund, Norway

This looks like the most elegant witches' lair in the world. In fact, it's the best of Norway's wonderful Stave churches – remarkable survivors of medieval woodwork.

Built between 1150 and 1350, the stave churches manage to mix the Christian and Viking traditions to winning effect; featuring wooden beams and flying dragons, and with elemental Fjordside locations, they make all who visit reach for their cameras.

© ALEKSANDRA H KOSSOWSKA / SHUTTERSTOCK

Arch of Septimius Severus

193–211AD

Septimius Severus
Leptis Magna, Libya

Libya doesn't have great press at the moment. But a couple of hundred years into the first millennium, local boy and emperor Septimius Severus made Leptis Magna one of the biggest and finest cities in the Mediterranean and the whole Roman Empire, with a huge forum, busy docks and this 'tetrapylon' four-way arch marking the crossing of two vital roads. Now Leptis Magna is a ruined city in Khoms, about 80 miles east of Tripoli, and Septimius's glorious arch – once a huge tourist draw – is in difficult territory.

Wall House II

1973–2001
John Hejduk
Groningen,
Netherlands

This pastel beauty is pride of place in the Dutch university town, and an essay in the mingling of form and colour. With curvaceous and colourful elements up against a large and slightly forbidding concrete wall, it's like a built version of a Cubist painting. It was drawn from an original unbuilt plan by Hejduk for an American house in 1973, then put on hold until a Dutch enthusiast decided to have a go. Although Wall House 2 is privately owned, the owners have a public area that can be visited.

© ZOONAR GMBH / ALAMY STOCK PHOTO

Stone House (Casa do Penedo)

1974
Architect N/A
Fafe, Portugal

Few houses respond to the landscape quite as closely as this family home in Portugal's mountainous interior. Taking full advantage of four massive boulders, and on an amazing hilltop site, the Stone House is so odd and delightful that tourists make their way here in droves – a fact that apparently caused the last owner to leave (although, as it's said to have bulletproof doors and windows, there may be other reasons). With a swimming hole nearby and a small museum within, it will continue to be the apex of a good hike.

Alhambra

1238

Architect N/A
Granada, Spain

The Alhambra started as a fort in the Moorish occupation of Spain. When Charles came back to re-conquer, it was changed forever – apart, that is, from the courtyard, fountains and flowing gardens. It's a world-class wonder for a relatively small town and almost didn't survive the 18th and 19th centuries, but now it's UNESCO-listed and houses two museums. But it's the whole gorgeous site that delights; or as the author Washington Irving put it: 'How unworthy is my scribbling of the place?'

© RAVI TAHILRAMANI / GETTY IMAGES

Shah Mosque

1611

Shaykh-i Bahāʾī
Esfahan, Iran

The Masjed-e-Shah, considered by many to be the finest mosque in Iran, is in the royal square of Isfahan, once the country's capital. With glittering mosaic tiles in seven colours and calligraphic inscriptions, it's one of the Islamic world's great buildings and a centrepiece of Iran's growing tourism industry.

Notable features include the four iwans or arcades, by which the Shah promoted a Persian architectural style, and with the dome you can enjoy a wondrous moment when a stamped foot creates seven echoes.

Colosseum

70–80AD

Vespasian, Titus
Rome, Italy

It's hard to think of the Colosseum without thinking of a swords and sandals epic starring say, Charlton Heston. And it's hard to enter this huge Roman ovoid without the clang of sword and the baying for blood in the mind's ear.

The Flavian Amphitheatre (as it's also known) is estimated to have held up to 80,000 spectators, and as you clamber over the stalls, remember that from here those spectators watched executions, animal hunts and re-enactments of famous battles right through to the medieval era.

© GALINA MIKHALISHINA / SHUTTERSTOCK

Field of Miracles

11th century–

**Bonanno Pisano,
Buscheto and others
Pisa, Italy**

It's thronged, and ridiculously touristy. But the Campo dei Miracoli (a term coined by poet Gabriele D'Annunzio) really is worth it. There's The Cathedral or Duomo, the Baptistry, the Monumental Cemetery, and of course, the Leaning Tower. The mixture of green grass and the white marble is exquisite and Pisa itself straddles the river Arno like a dream (indeed, it's the riverine marshes that make the ground unstable and caused that fateful lean). Come on a winter morning and you'll see a dreamscape – yes, a miraculous one.

Gallarus Oratory

700–800AD

Architect N/A
Dingle, Kerry, Ireland

Why this humble bothy? Because, in its frugal stone and story of early Christianity, it's an icon of northern European building. Often compared to an upturned boat (this is the wuthering Atlantic coast, after all) it's satisfyingly simple: a dry-stone church with an entrance and an east window. Both its date and its use are contested by historians, but nothing detracts from the Oratory's pleasing simplicity.

Skara Brae

3200BC–2200BC
Architect N/A
Orkneys, Scotland

At many archaeological sites, numinous as they are, you don't get a sense of how those old-timers lived. But at Skara Brae, you do. Here, in Europe's best-kept Neolithic settlement – eight houses in all – you'll find furniture, gaming dice, tools and jewellery made more than 5000 years ago.

It was only through the serendipity of a storm in 1850 that we even have Skara Brae, once a hillock. Thought to be Iron Age, radiocarbon dating pushed it back to the late Neolithic. But when you see the square room, with a central fireplace, a bed, a dresser on the wall opposite the doorway, you'll certainly think *plus ca change*.

Palazzo Te

1524–34
Giulio Romano
Mantua, Italy

'Get thee to Mantua' said Shakespeare in *Romeo and Juliet*, and it's still good advice. For here, you'll find the Palazzo Te, with hall after gobsmacking hall of frescoes, painted ceilings and marble floors: Palazzo Te meant 'the abode of the Gods', and local ruler

Mantova II Gonzaga wanted his palace to be the coolest place in the region, hiring painter and architect Giulio Romano, a pupil of Raphael, to do the honours. It's now a temple to Mannerism, the florid late-renaissance style, with each space opening the jaw a little wider.

Towers of San Gimignano

13th–14th centuries

Architect N/A
Tuscany, Italy

Long ago, many years before Manhattan, there was a small town in Italy that had a thing for towers. It's though that San Gimignano started to build towers because of local rivalries, and it just grew, with families building towers higher than the proverbial Jones's next door. Once there were 72 tower houses, up to 70m high. Devastated after the Black Death, the town was rediscovered as a tourist trap in the 19th century, and although only 14 towers remain, it's still a remarkable memento of sky-reaching ambition.

Roman Baths

Roman origin 60–70AD:
remade 1894–7

**John Wood, the Elder,
John Wood, the Younger
Bath, UK**

Never has water cascaded down the ages so exquisitely. Once the Roman city of Aquae Sulis ('the waters of Sulis') the golden-stoned city of Bath is the finest Georgian set-piece in the world, and the Roman Baths its centrepiece. They include the central Sacred Spring, surrounded by Georgian splendour from master builders John Wood the Elder and Younger, and the Temple, the Bath House, and a museum. You can't swim in the baths' frightening green water – but its sulphurous smell will likely put you off, in any case.

Dome of the Rock

687–691AD

**Caliph Abd al-Malik
Jerusalem, Israel
(administered
by Jordan)**

It's a contested spot – but undeniably beautiful.

Oiginally dating from the 7th century, the Dome of the Rock is said to be the first domed shrine, over an octagonal plan and rotunda that draws from the Byzantine tradition. The golden dome is an eternal edifice, like a rising or setting sun, and the surface decoration hits the spot with Ottoman era tiles marble and mosaic – and that gold, redone in 1994.

© JCARILLET / GETTY IMAGES

Hallgrímur church

1945

Guðjón Samúelsson
Reykjavík, Iceland

This astonishing church is the centrepiece of Rekyavik: its sentinel, mascot and sanctuary. Coming on like a rocket, its skyward concrete thrust never fails to impress. Named after the 17th-century clergyman Hallgrímur Pétursson, Samuel was inspired by the basalt in the Icelandic landscape, which cools to form organ pipe-like flutes. Indeed, within is a vast pipe organ and there's an organ festival every year. History buffs will like the statue Leifur Eiriksson (c 970–c1020) – the first European to discover America in 1000AD. Don't dare to contradict this.

© TAKEPICSFORFUN / GETTY IMAGES

Monastery of Geghard

4th–13th centuries
St Gregory the Illuminator
Goght, Armenia

A church cut into rock is an eternal sight and this, the monastery of Geghard in Armenia's Upper Azat Valley, has several in a medieval complex. The Monastery began as a small cave chapel, which Gregory declared held a sacred spring in the 4th century, and perhaps due in part to its awesome location, with looming cliffs and the Azat river gorge, became the ecclesiastical and cultural centre of medieval Armenia. The name 'Geghard' refers to the spear that wounded Christ, and Dan Brownites will enjoy the fact that the spear remains here.

Old Mosque City of Bagerhat

15th century
Ulugh Khan Jahan
Bagerhat, Bangladesh

Not so many tourists come to Bangladesh. But perhaps they should, particularly to see the Mosque City of Bagerhat. It's where the Ganges and Brahmaputra rivers meet, and still a trading post – but it's the ancient city, founded by a Turkish general, that's the reason to come. With 81 domes and more than 60 pillars, it's a classic example of the baked brickwork or terracotta of Muslim Bengal, with artificial tusks of elephants decorating the exteriors of the minarets.

© DANITA DELIMONT / GETTY IMAGES

Fasil Ghebbi

1636–

**Emperor Fasilides
Gondar, Ethiopia**

Once a menagerie of beasts was kept at this imperial royal enclosure of Ethiopia in Gondar. They're no longer here, but the whole complex is recognisable as the estate of an extremely powerful ruler. It's a fortified palace in a style a Westerner would understand, thanks to the baroque style brought by Jesuit missionaries, yet with Nubian, Hindu and Arabic influences in the decoration and domes. On the high plateau of northern Ethiopia near Lake Tana, it's a big stop on Ethiopia's 'golden triangle'.

Agadez mosque

1515, restored 1844
Architect N/A
Agadez, Niger

This is the tallest structure made of mud – or rather, adobe – in the world. The mosque and its 27m-high minaret are, amazingly, built from a robust mix of mud, straw and pebbles, which gives it the deliciously rounded look, and it's been here since the 14th century, when it was built as the residence of the Sultan of Agadez, leader of local Tuaregs. Rain isn't good for it – hence the strengthening beams that give it its distinctive façade – but it's sturdy enough that you can walk up it, if you're ready for a hot climb. You'll find it on the southern side of the Sahara.

Bahla Fort

12th–15th centuries
Architect N/A
Bahlat, Oman

Bahla Fort is one of the oldest and biggest in Oman, and a gem: a huge edifice of mud, brick and stone in the Bahla oasis. Round towers, wells, castellations and miles of walls testify to a great cultural monument, augmented by timber doors, shelves and window screens – and you'll want to rock the Al Qabasah, a splendid five-storey collection of rooms. It's been renewed several times: the last time was 2012.

Jongmyo shrine

1394

King Taejo
Seoul, South Korea

Chosen for its understated charms – just look at those eaves – Jongmyo is a royal shrine for the ancestral Joseon dynasty. So it's muted and elegant. At 109m. the main hall is one of the world's longest single wooden structures, and Jongmyo's purpose was to honour his ancestors properly, with no undue ornamentation and a real sense of minimalist dignity.